Introducing Continents

Australia

Anita Ganeri

Heinemann
LIBRARY

Chicago, Illinois

© 2014 Heinemann Library
an imprint of Capstone Global Library, LLC
Chicago, Illinois

To contact Capstone Global Library please phone 800-747-4992, or visit our web site, www.capstonepub.com

Edited by Dan Nunn, Rebecca Rissman, Sian Smith, and Helen Cox Cannons
Designed by Philippa Jenkins
Original illustrations © Capstone Global Library Ltd 2014
Picture research by Liz Alexander and Tristan Leverett
Production by Vicki Fitzgerald
Originated by Capstone Global Library Ltd

Library of Congress Cataloging-in-Publication Data
Ganeri, Anita, 1961-
  Introducing Australia / Anita Ganeri.
    pages cm.—(Introducing continents)
  Includes bibliographical references and index.
  ISBN 978-1-4329-8041-2 (hb)—ISBN 978-1-4329-8049-8 (pb) 1. Australia—Juvenile literature. I. Title.

  DU96.G36 2013
  994—dc23   2012049493

Acknowledgments
The author and publisher are grateful to the following for permission to reproduce copyright material: Alamy Stock Photo: Bill Bachman, 18, Paul Kingsley, 21, Steffan Hill, 13; Getty Images: Danita Delimont, 25, Jason Edwards, 10, Marianna Massey, 23, Martin Cohen/Wild About Australia, 12, Pawel Toczynski, 9, Quinn Rooney, 22, SHARON SMITH/AFP, 20, TED MEAD, 8; Kit Kittle: 27; Nature Picture Library: Doug Perrine, 15, Ingo Arndt, 14; Shutterstock: Alberto Loyo, 11, Alexander Hoffmann, 19 Bottom, AridOcean, Cover (map), Ashley Whitworth, 17, Phillip Minnis, 26, Ralph Loesche, Cover Top, Susan Harris, 6, Szekeres Szabolcs, 16; SuperStock: age fotostock, 7, Robert Harding Picture Library, Cover Bottom, Robin Smith, 19 Top.

Every effort has been made to contact copyright holders of any material reproduced in this book. Any omissions will be rectified in subsequent printings if notice is given to the publisher.

Disclaimer

Contents

Some words are shown in bold, **like this**. You can find out what they mean by looking in the glossary.

About Australia

A **continent** is a huge area of land. There are seven continents on Earth. This book is about the continent of Australia. Australia is the world's smallest continent.

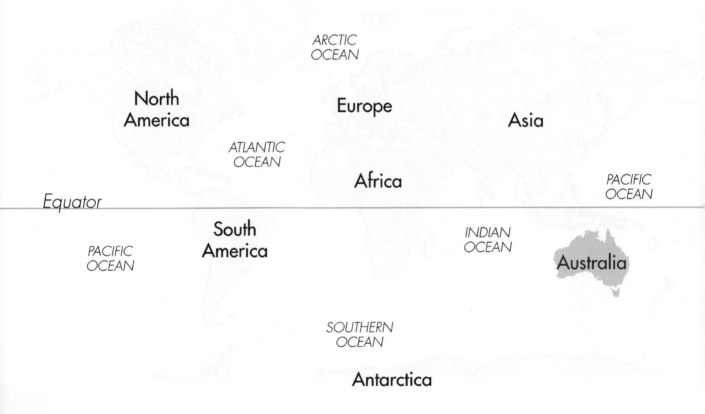

ARCTIC OCEAN

North America

Europe

Asia

ATLANTIC OCEAN

Africa

PACIFIC OCEAN

Equator

PACIFIC OCEAN

South America

INDIAN OCEAN

Australia

SOUTHERN OCEAN

Antarctica

Australia is a huge island. It is surrounded by the Indian Ocean and the Pacific Ocean. Australia also includes the island of Tasmania to the south.

Australia Fact File	
Area	2,966,136 square miles (7,713,364 square kilometers)
Population	22 million
Number of countries	1
Highest mountain	Mount Kosciuszko at 7,310 feet (2,228 meters)
Longest river	Murray-Darling at 2,376 miles (3,824 kilometers)

Famous Places

There are many famous places in Australia. Some are modern. The Sydney Opera House opened in 1973. It has become one of the most famous buildings in the world. Its roof looks like a ship's sails.

The Sydney Opera House stands in Sydney Harbor.

Uluru stands 1,100 feet (335 meters) high. It used to be called Ayers Rock.

Some famous places are very old. Uluru is a giant hill of red rock in central Australia. It is a **sacred** place for the **Aboriginal** people. It has many caves and ancient rock paintings.

Geography

Huge, dry **deserts** cover large parts of western and central Australia. The biggest is the Great Victoria Desert. It is famous for its red **sand dunes**.

The Great Victoria Desert has sand dunes, pebbly plains, and salt lakes.

INDIAN OCEAN

PACIFIC OCEAN

Great Sandy Desert

Hamersley Range

Great Dividing Range

Great Victoria Desert

Mount Kosciuszko

0   200 miles
0   320 km

TASMAN SEA

Mount Kosciuszko is in the Snowy Mountains in southeast Australia.

A long line of mountains runs down the eastern side of Australia. It is called the Great Dividing Range. To the south is the highest mountain in Australia—Mount Kosciuszko. It is 7,310 feet (2,228 meters) tall.

The Murray and Darling rivers join up to make the Murray-Darling River. It is the longest river in Australia. It flows for 2,376 miles (3,824 kilometers) from the Great Dividing Range into the ocean.

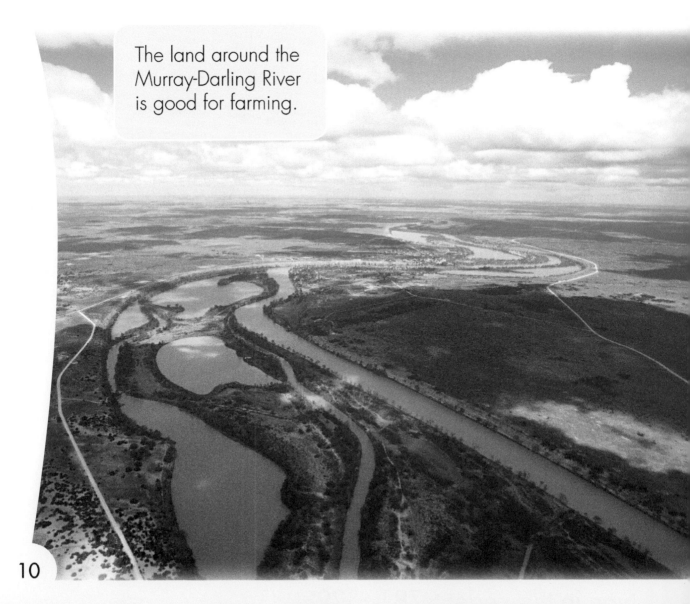

The land around the Murray-Darling River is good for farming.

Lake Eyre looks almost empty here. It fills up again after heavy rains.

Lake Eyre is the biggest lake in Australia. It is filled with **salt water**, but often dries out in the heat. The lake has only been full of water three times in the last 100 years.

Weather

Most of Australia has hot, dry weather. When it is very dry, there is a risk of Bushfires breaking out. The far north and northeast have warm weather with lots of rain.

Bushfires spread very quickly if the ground is dry.

In Australia, Christmas is in the summer time. Some Australians spend Christmas on the beach.

Australia is in the Southern Hemisphere. It has opposite seasons to the Northern Hemisphere. Winter lasts from June to August. Summer lasts from December to February.

Animals

Australia's most famous animals are **marsupials**, such as koalas and kangaroos. These are animals that carry their babies in pouches. Many unusual birds also live in Australia, such as kookaburras and emus.

A kangaroo carries its baby, or joey, in its pouch.

Thousands of multicolored fish swim on the Great Barrier Reef.

The Great Barrier Reef stretches along the northeast coast of Australia. It is the biggest **coral reef** on Earth. It is home to an astonishing number of animals. They include around 1,500 types of fish.

Plants

Many unusual plants grow in Australia. Eucalyptus trees, sometimes called gum trees, grow all over the **continent**. Their leaves make a strong-smelling oil. Eucalyptus leaves are the favorite food of koalas.

Koalas eat so many eucalyptus leaves that they smell of eucalyptus.

The seeds of the Sturt's desert pea can sprout very quickly after a shower of rain.

The Sturt's desert pea is a plant that grows in the **desert**. It has bunches of bright red and black flowers. Its seeds lie in the hot ground. They grow very quickly as soon as it rains.

Natural Resources

Australia has many **natural resources**. About two-thirds of the land is used for farming. In the dry **outback**, farmers keep sheep on enormous farms. The sheep are mainly kept for their wool.

These merino sheep are raised for their soft, fine wool.

This digger is working on an opal mine in Australia.

Many metals, such as gold and iron **ore**, are **mined** in Australia. There are also huge diamond mines. Most of the world's **opals** come from Australia. The **continent** is also rich in oil, gas, and coal.

polished opal

People

About 22 million people live in Australia. Most people are **descended from** Europeans who settled in Australia. Other people have come from Asian countries, such as China and Vietnam.

These Australian schoolchildren come from many different backgrounds.

These Aboriginal children are dressed in traditional costumes for a dance.

The **Aboriginals** were the first people to live in Australia. They came from Southeast Asia around 40,000 years ago. They used to move from place to place, but now many live in cities and towns.

Sports and Culture

Sports are very popular in Australia. Many Australians play or watch cricket, rugby, and Australian rules football. Australian rules football is played on an oval-shaped field. It is like a cross between rugby and soccer.

These men are playing Australian rules football in Melbourne.

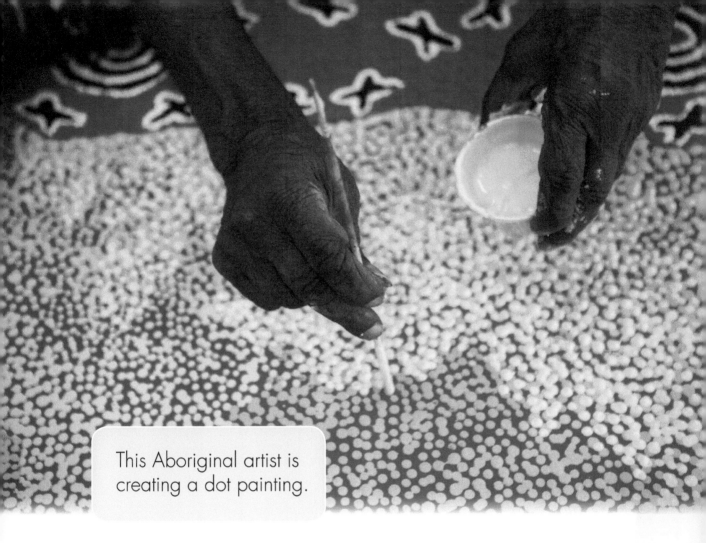

This Aboriginal artist is creating a dot painting.

The **Aboriginal** people have their own art and music that is thousands of years old. They paint pictures using dots of different colors. The paintings usually show animals or pictures from Aboriginal stories.

Countries

There is just one country in the **continent** of Australia and that is Australia! Australia is divided into six **states** and two **territories**. The largest Australian state is Western Australia.

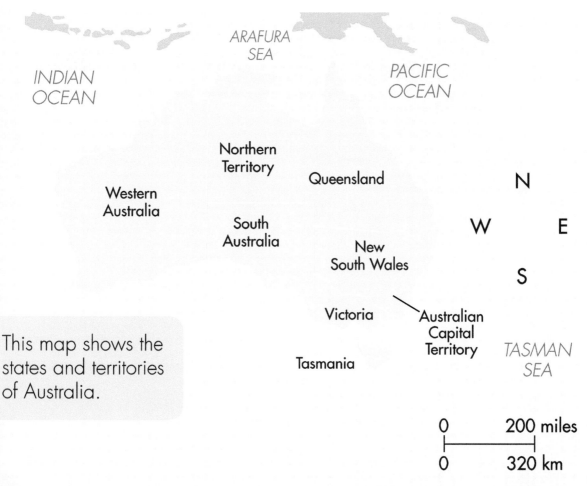

ARAFURA SEA

INDIAN OCEAN

PACIFIC OCEAN

Northern Territory

Queensland

N

Western Australia

South Australia

W

E

New South Wales

S

Victoria

Australian Capital Territory

TASMAN SEA

Tasmania

This map shows the states and territories of Australia.

0 — 200 miles

0 — 320 km

This is one of the islands that make up Fiji in the South Pacific Ocean.

Australia is part of a much bigger region called Oceania. Oceania also includes New Zealand, Papua New Guinea, and thousands of islands in the South Pacific Ocean.

Cities and Countryside

There are many big, modern cities in Australia. Canberra is the capital of Australia. It is home to the Australian **parliament**. Sydney is the biggest city. It is famous for its harbor and harbor bridge.

The famous harbor bridge in Sydney is made from steel.

A "flying doctor" arrives at the scene of a car accident.

People in the **outback** often live far away from cities and towns. If people get sick or have an accident, a "flying doctor" goes out to visit them in a plane. Some children living in the outback have to do their schoolwork by radio or on the computer.

Fun Facts

- Australia is a huge island. It is also a **continent** and a country.

- Eight of the world's ten most deadly snakes live in Australia.

- In Australia, there are about three sheep for every one person.

- More than three-quarters of Australians live in towns and cities.

Quiz

1. What is the capital of Australia?

2. Who were the first people to live in Australia?

3. Does Australia lie above or below the equator?

4. Name two types of **marsupials**.

4. Kangaroos and koalas

3. Below

2. Aboriginals

1. Canberra

Glossary

Aboriginal first people to live in Australia

continent one of seven huge areas of land on Earth

coral reef rocky structure built by tiny sea creatures

descended from related to someone long ago

desert hot, dry place that has very little rain

marsupials animals that carry their young in pouches

mined dug up from under the ground

natural resources natural materials that we use, such as wood, coal, oil, and rock

opal type of precious stone

ore rock that contains metals

outback dry land in the middle of Australia

parliament group of people that makes a country's laws

sacred special or holy

salt water water that is salty, like the ocean

sand dunes huge piles of sand in the desert

states areas of Australia that make their own laws

territories areas of Australia with their own laws

Find Out More

Books

Bingham, Jane. *Exploring Australia*. Chicago: Heinemann, 2007.

Niz, Xavier. *Spotlight on Australia*. Mankato, Minn.: Capstone, 2011.

Royston, Angela and Michael Scott. *Australia's Most Amazing Plants*. Chicago: Raintree, 2009.

Websites

FactHound offers a safe, fun way to find Internet sites related to this book. All of the sites on FactHound have been researched by our staff.

Here's all you do:
Visit www.facthound.com
Type in this code: 9781432980412

Index